Easy Password Tracker

Site	Username	Password

Easy Password Tracker

Site	Username	Password

Easy Password Tracker

Site	Username	Password

Easy Password Tracker

Site	Username	Password

Easy Password Tracker

Site	Username	Password

Easy Password Tracker

Site	Username	Password

Easy Password Tracker

Site	Username	Password

Easy Password Tracker

Site	Username	Password

Easy Password Tracker

Site	Username	Password

Easy Password Tracker

Site	Username	Password

Easy Password Tracker

Site	Username	Password

Easy Password Tracker

Site	Username	Password

Easy Password Tracker

Site	Username	Password

Easy Password Tracker

Site	Username	Password

Easy Password Tracker

Site	Username	Password

Easy Password Tracker

Site	Username	Password

Easy Password Tracker

Site	Username	Password

Easy Password Tracker

Site	Username	Password

Easy Password Tracker

Site	Username	Password

Easy Password Tracker

Site	Username	Password

Easy Password Tracker

Site	Username	Password

Easy Password Tracker

Site	Username	Password

Easy Password Tracker

Site	Username	Password

Easy Password Tracker

Site	Username	Password

Easy Password Tracker

Site	Username	Password

Easy Password Tracker

Site	Username	Password

Easy Password Tracker

Site	Username	Password

Easy Password Tracker

Site	Username	Password

Easy Password Tracker

Site	Username	Password

Easy Password Tracker

Site	Username	Password

Easy Password Tracker

Site	Username	Password

Easy Password Tracker

Site	Username	Password

Easy Password Tracker

Site	Username	Password

Easy Password Tracker

Site	Username	Password

Easy Password Tracker

Site	Username	Password

Easy Password Tracker

Site	Username	Password

Easy Password Tracker

Site	Username	Password

Easy Password Tracker

Site	Username	Password

Easy Password Tracker

Site	Username	Password

Easy Password Tracker

Site	Username	Password

Easy Password Tracker

Site	Username	Password

Easy Password Tracker

Site	Username	Password

Easy Password Tracker

Site	Username	Password

Easy Password Tracker

Site	Username	Password

Easy Password Tracker

Site	Username	Password

Easy Password Tracker

Site	Username	Password

Easy Password Tracker

Site	Username	Password

Easy Password Tracker

Site	Username	Password

Easy Password Tracker

Site	Username	Password

Easy Password Tracker

Site	Username	Password